CHINESE MYTHS

Jane Bingham

W

FRANKLIN WATTS

LONDON·SYDNEY

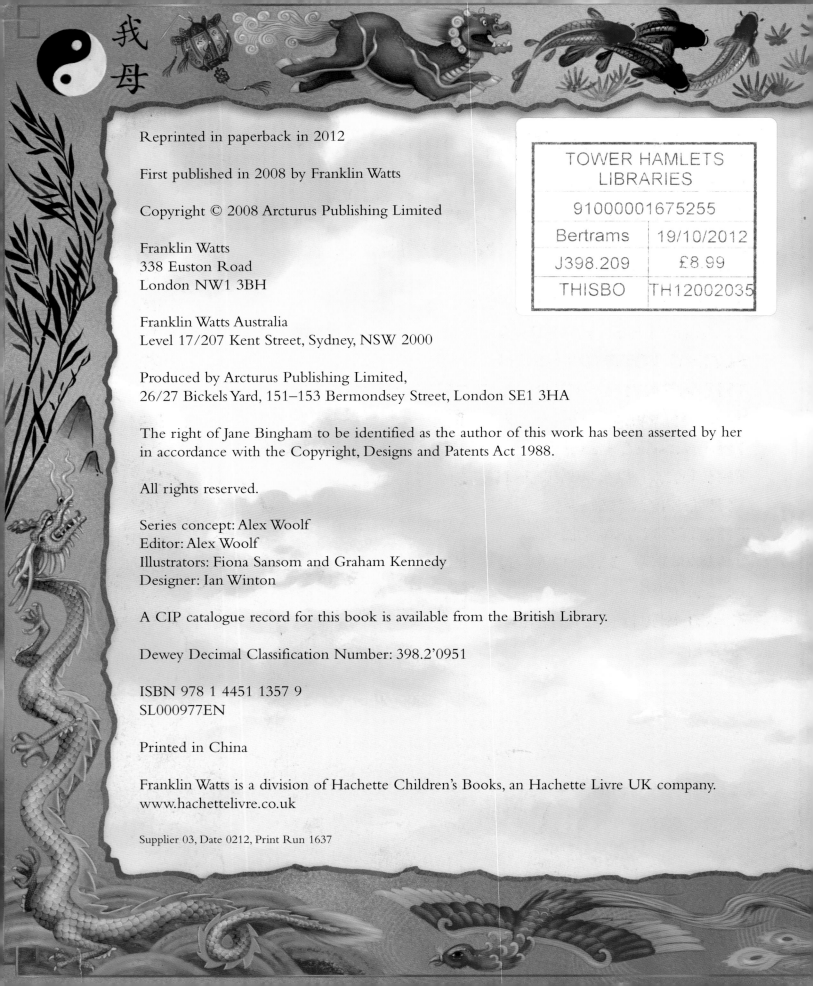

Reprinted in paperback in 2012

First published in 2008 by Franklin Watts

Copyright © 2008 Arcturus Publishing Limited

Franklin Watts
338 Euston Road
London NW1 3BH

Franklin Watts Australia
Level 17/207 Kent Street, Sydney, NSW 2000

Produced by Arcturus Publishing Limited,
26/27 Bickels Yard, 151–153 Bermondsey Street, London SE1 3HA

The right of Jane Bingham to be identified as the author of this work has been asserted by her
in accordance with the Copyright, Designs and Patents Act 1988.

Series concept: Alex Woolf
Editor: Alex Woolf
Illustrators: Fiona Sansom and Graham Kennedy
Designer: Ian Winton

A CIP catalogue record for this book is available from the British Library.

Dewey Decimal Classification Number: 398.2'0951

ISBN 978 1 4451 1357 9
SL000977EN

Printed in China

Franklin Watts is a division of Hachette Children's Books, an Hachette Livre UK company.
www.hachettelivre.co.uk

Supplier 03, Date 0212, Print Run 1637

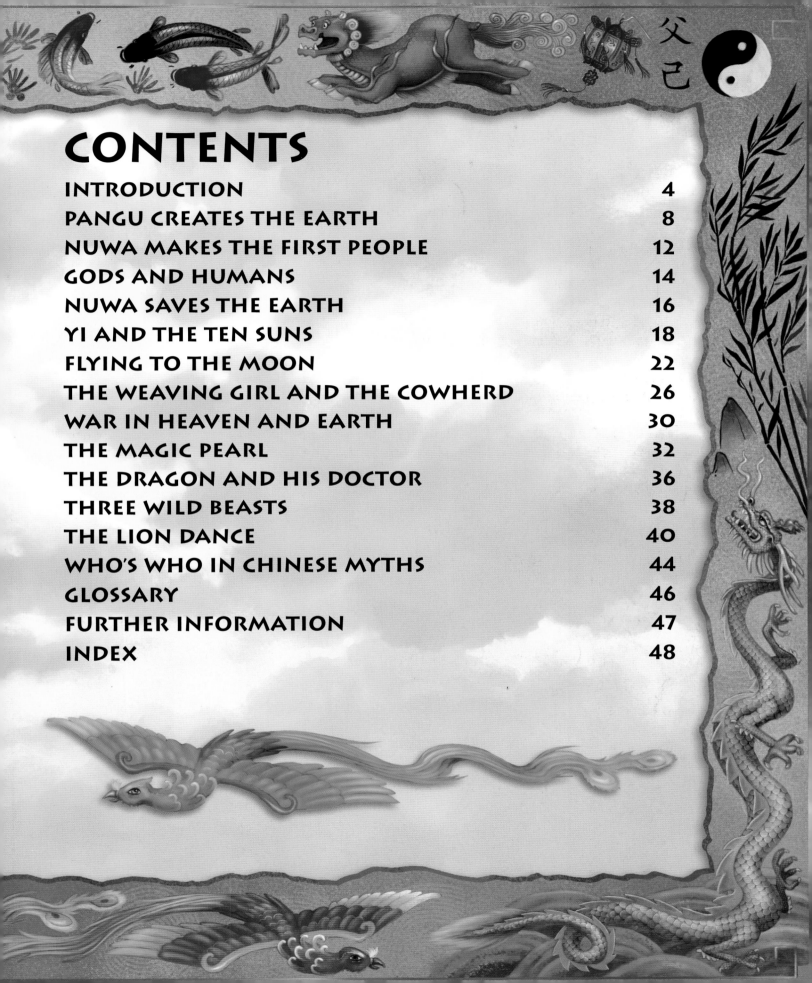

CONTENTS

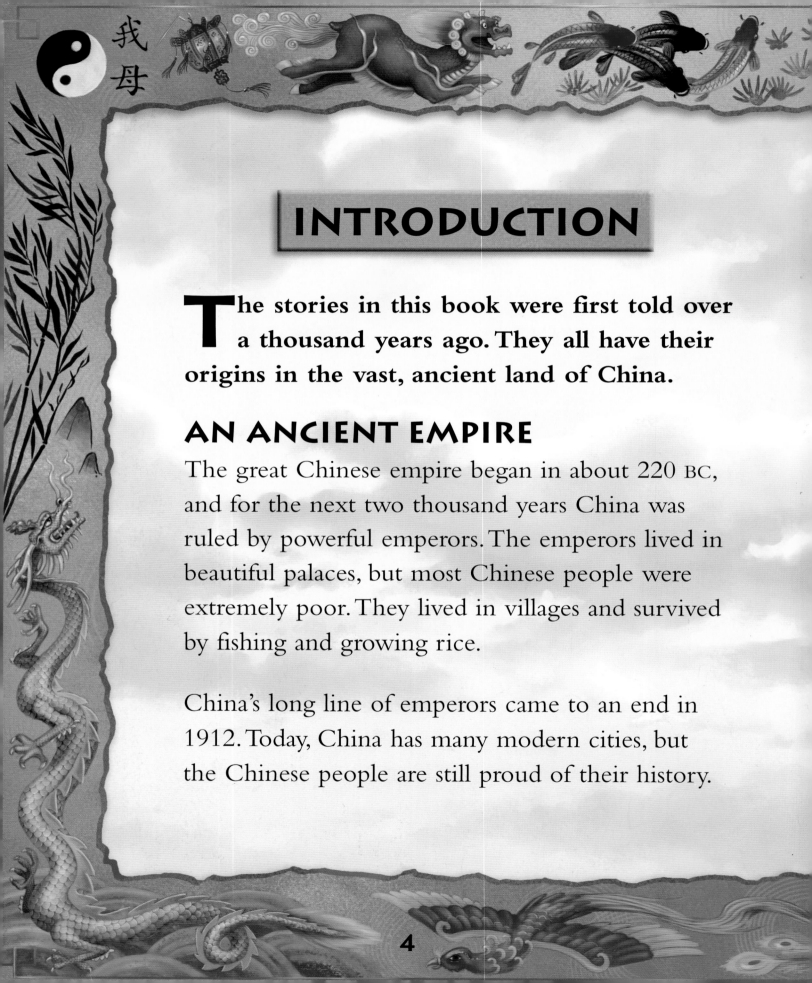

INTRODUCTION

The stories in this book were first told over a thousand years ago. They all have their origins in the vast, ancient land of China.

AN ANCIENT EMPIRE

The great Chinese empire began in about 220 BC, and for the next two thousand years China was ruled by powerful emperors. The emperors lived in beautiful palaces, but most Chinese people were extremely poor. They lived in villages and survived by fishing and growing rice.

China's long line of emperors came to an end in 1912. Today, China has many modern cities, but the Chinese people are still proud of their history.

HUANG HO

KAIFENG •

CHANG'AN •

• LO-YANG

HANGCHOW •

YELLOW
SEA

YANGTZE KIANG

CHINA

SOUTH CHINA
SEA

N

W   E

S

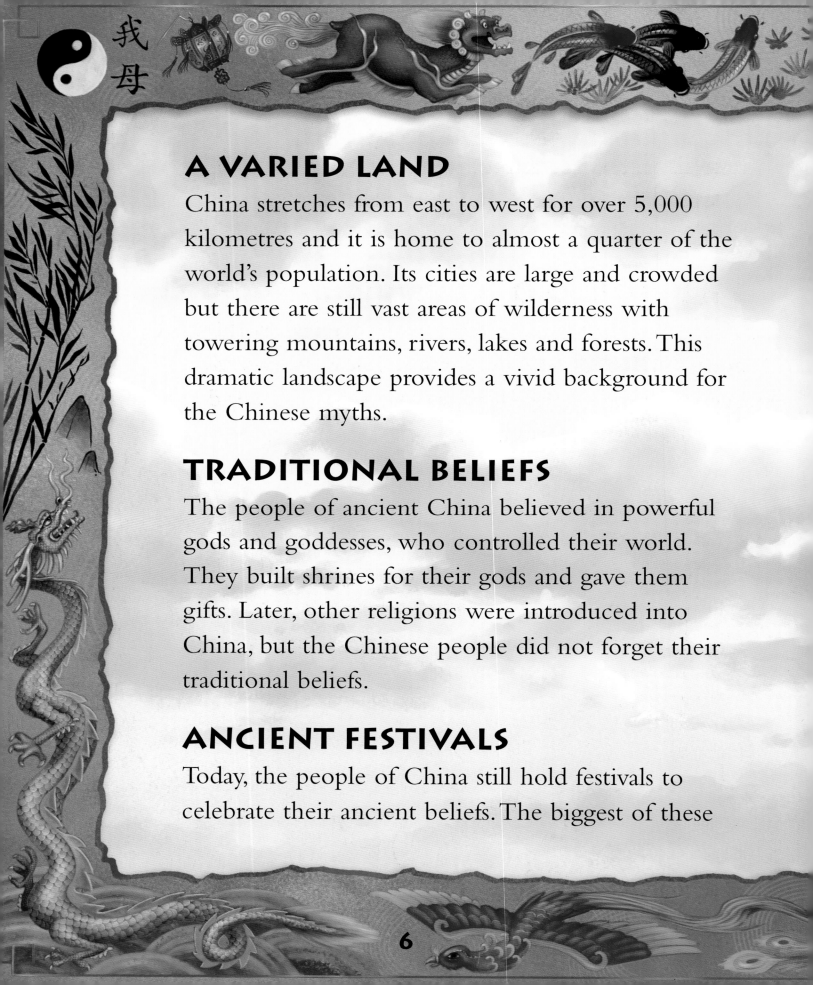

A VARIED LAND

China stretches from east to west for over 5,000 kilometres and it is home to almost a quarter of the world's population. Its cities are large and crowded but there are still vast areas of wilderness with towering mountains, rivers, lakes and forests. This dramatic landscape provides a vivid background for the Chinese myths.

TRADITIONAL BELIEFS

The people of ancient China believed in powerful gods and goddesses, who controlled their world. They built shrines for their gods and gave them gifts. Later, other religions were introduced into China, but the Chinese people did not forget their traditional beliefs.

ANCIENT FESTIVALS

Today, the people of China still hold festivals to celebrate their ancient beliefs. The biggest of these festivals takes place at New Year. People dress up in colourful costumes and perform a lion dance through the streets.

THE WORLD OF CHINESE MYTHS

The myths in this book are set in a magical world of gods, spirits and dragons. Some tell how the world began. Others explain features of the natural world such as rivers and mountains.

Many of the myths teach a lesson about the way people should live. In these stories, men and women are punished for their selfish actions and rewarded when they are honest and kind. These ancient Chinese myths still have a message for us today.

PANGU CREATES THE EARTH

In the beginning, the universe was a giant egg, floating in a misty cloud. Inside the egg were two powerful forces: a female force called Yin, and a male force called Yang. Together, these two forces created the giant, Pangu.

After thousands of years asleep inside the egg Pangu gradually started to wake up. He uncurled his massive body and pushed hard against the sides of the egg. As Pangu pushed, the egg broke apart. The heavy Yin parts sank down and formed the earth. The light Yang parts rose up and became the sky.

Pangu stood between the earth and the sky, pushing them apart. Each day he grew taller,

and the sky
and earth stretched
further apart.
For thousands
of years, Pangu
pushed as hard as he
could. Then one day
he realized that his
work was over.
It was time for
him to lie down
and rest.

Pangu was exhausted after his efforts and he curled up on the earth to die. But this was not the end of the great giant. Slowly, his body was transformed into the features of our earth and sky.

After Pangu's death, his massive arms and legs became the earth's mountains. His blood became the water in the rivers, lakes, and oceans, and his veins became the paths crossing the land. Pangu's skin stretched over the surface of the earth to create its soil, and all the flowers and trees on earth grew from the hairs on his body.

High up in the sky, Pangu's shining eyes became the sun and moon, and the millions of hairs on his head turned into the stars. His breath was the wind and clouds, and his sweat was the rain. Pangu's booming voice was heard every time the thunder rolled.

Pangu had created a beautiful world, but something was missing. There were no people to enjoy his creation.

NUWA MAKES THE FIRST PEOPLE

While Pangu was busy creating the world, five great emperor gods were ruling the heavens. One of the gods had a younger sister called Nuwa. She was a lively, restless spirit and she often visited the earth looking for adventure.

Nuwa thought the earth was a marvellous place, but she was lonely wandering there alone. So one day she amused herself by moulding a small figure out of clay. She shaped her model just like an emperor god, with a tiny head, legs and arms. Then she put him on the earth to see if he would stand.

As soon as his feet touched the earth, the little figure began to dance and sing. Nuwa was delighted, and she quickly started moulding other figures, some shaped like gods and others like goddesses. Soon, the giant goddess was surrounded by tiny men and women, all dancing and singing together. She had created the first human beings.

GODS AND HUMANS

The first humans found life on earth very difficult. They lived in caves and survived by gathering food, but they were often cold and hungry.

The gods were sad to see humans suffering, so they decided to give them some help. One god taught people how to build shelters. Another showed them how to grow crops, and a third taught them how to create fire. All these valuable lessons made life on earth much easier.

The Blue Emperor god Fushi was a great friend to human beings. He taught them to make bows and arrows and fishing nets and showed them how to play music on a bamboo pipe.

One god gave
a special gift to humans.
His name was Canjie and he
had four eyes to help him keep
the heavenly records. Canjie
made simple drawings of
everything on earth. Then he
taught people how to draw
these symbols. Over the
centuries, the picture symbols
became much simpler to
draw. This was the start of
Chinese writing.

NUWA SAVES THE EARTH

For many years, men and women lived peacefully on the earth. But then something terrible happened. The sky split open, releasing torrents of rain, and the earth was soon covered with swirling water. Meanwhile, the mountains erupted in flames, and boiling lava poured down their sides.

The earth was in danger of being completely destroyed. But Nuwa was determined to save her people. She chose five beautifully coloured stones and heated them in a fire. Then she used the stones to mend the cracks in the sky.

Once the sky was mended, Nuwa stopped the floods by building dams and lakes all over the earth. Next, she killed a giant turtle and cut off its legs. She used the turtle's sturdy legs to make four pillars to support the sky.

Now Nuwa felt confident that her precious humans would be safe. She said goodbye to the other gods and disappeared forever.

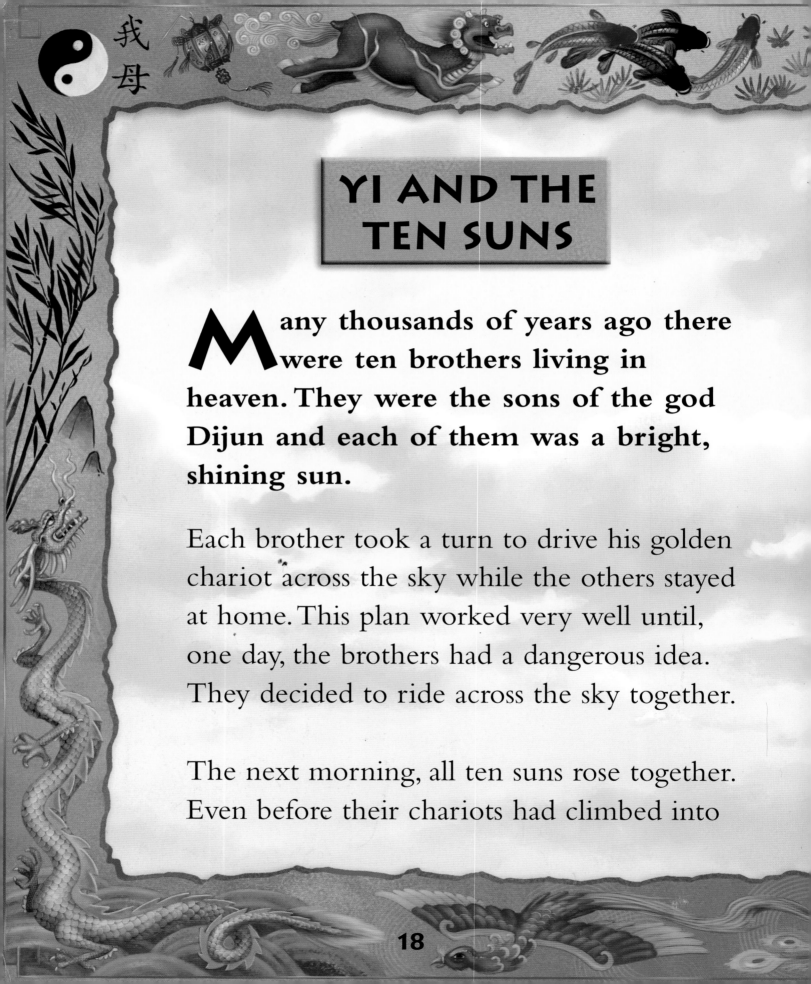

YI AND THE TEN SUNS

Many thousands of years ago there were ten brothers living in heaven. They were the sons of the god Dijun and each of them was a bright, shining sun.

Each brother took a turn to drive his golden chariot across the sky while the others stayed at home. This plan worked very well until, one day, the brothers had a dangerous idea. They decided to ride across the sky together.

The next morning, all ten suns rose together. Even before their chariots had climbed into

the sky, the earth began to bake. Crops in the fields withered and died and rivers and lakes dried up. People and animals bellowed in pain as ten suns beat down on their heads and the burning ground scorched their feet.

When Dijun realized what his sons had done, he was very angry. He quickly summoned Yi, the heavenly archer. Yi was a great hunter and he was the only spirit who could save the earth.

Dijun told Yi that he must shoot at his sons and frighten them, but Yi knew that this would not be enough. The only way to save the earth was to kill Dijun's sons.

Yi strode out into the blinding heat, raised his bow and took careful aim at one of the suns. The next minute a shower of black feathers fell to earth – all that remained of the spirit of the sun. Eight more times, Yi took aim and shot straight at a sun, and eight times the black feathers fell to earth.

In the end there was just one sun left in the sky, giving exactly the right amount of heat and light. All the humans were happy because their earth had been saved, but Yi and Dijun were very sad. Dijun missed his sons terribly and he could not bear the sight of Yi in heaven. So Yi was banished from heaven and sent to live on earth.

FLYING TO THE MOON

Yi, the heavenly archer, soon became used to living on the earth. He married a beautiful woman called Chang Er and he had everything he wanted. However, one thing still troubled him. He did not want to die, as humans do. So he travelled to the top of the Jade Mountain to ask the Queen of the West for help.

The Queen of the West admired the brave archer who had saved the people of the earth, so she gave Yi a magic potion.

She explained that if he drank it at the moment of his death, he would rise straight up to heaven.

Yi hid the potion in his house and told no one about it except his wife. He loved Chang Er very much and he trusted her to keep his secret. However, Chang Er was not as trustworthy as Yi had imagined. She had always wanted to fly and, like Yi, she wanted to live forever.

Chang Er often thought about the hidden potion and wondered how it would feel to fly. Then one day she met a fortune-teller. The fortune-teller told her that she would leave the world that night and fly to a place where she would be happy forever.

Chang Er hurried home and took the potion. Then she felt herself drift up into the air and fly up to the moon. But when she reached the moon, she had a nasty surprise. She had turned into a horny toad!

When Yi discovered what his wife had done, he was very sad. But the gods took pity on him. After Yi died, he was allowed to return to heaven. Meanwhile, Chang Er was not shown any mercy. She had to spend eternity as a toad on the face of the moon. And if you look at the full moon very carefully, you can still see her crouching there.

THE WEAVING GIRL AND THE COWHERD

All the goddesses in heaven were beautiful, but the weaving girl was the loveliest of them all. She was the favourite granddaughter of Xuan Yuan, the mighty Yellow Emperor god.

Every day, the weaving girl took her loom to the banks of the river dividing heaven from earth. Then, one day, she saw a handsome cowherd on the opposite riverbank. After that, the couple met every day and they soon fell in love.

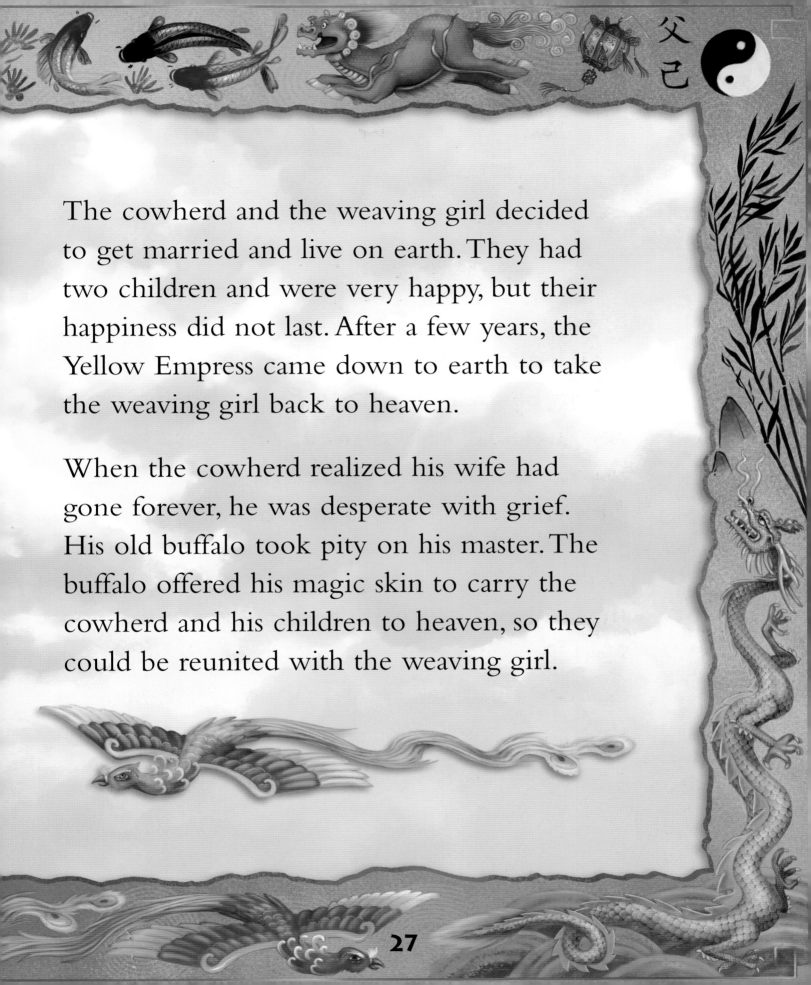

The cowherd and the weaving girl decided to get married and live on earth. They had two children and were very happy, but their happiness did not last. After a few years, the Yellow Empress came down to earth to take the weaving girl back to heaven.

When the cowherd realized his wife had gone forever, he was desperate with grief. His old buffalo took pity on his master. The buffalo offered his magic skin to carry the cowherd and his children to heaven, so they could be reunited with the weaving girl.

The cowherd had just reached the edge of heaven when the Yellow Empress spotted him. Swiftly, she pulled out her golden hairpin and drew a river of stars across the sky.

The river became the Milky Way, dividing heaven from earth. Now the cowherd could never reach his wife.

When the Yellow Emperor saw how sad the parted lovers were, he took pity on them. For just one night a year, he allowed the family to be together. On that night, the Yellow Emperor gave orders that all the magpies in the world should fly up to heaven and form a bridge across the river of stars.

If you look up at the sky at night, you will see two bright stars on either side of the Milky Way. Chinese people say the stars are the weaving girl and the cowherd, divided by a river of stars. For just one night each summer, the two stars seem to move closer together. That is the happy night when the lovers meet on the magpie bridge.

WAR IN HEAVEN AND EARTH

For thousands of years, the gods and humans were very happy. Gods often travelled to earth to help men and women, and humans came to heaven to ask the gods for advice. But then everything changed, and there were terrible wars in heaven and earth.

In heaven, the gods used armies of men to fight for them, and they also made men fight each other on earth. Millions of humans were killed, and the earth was in ruins.

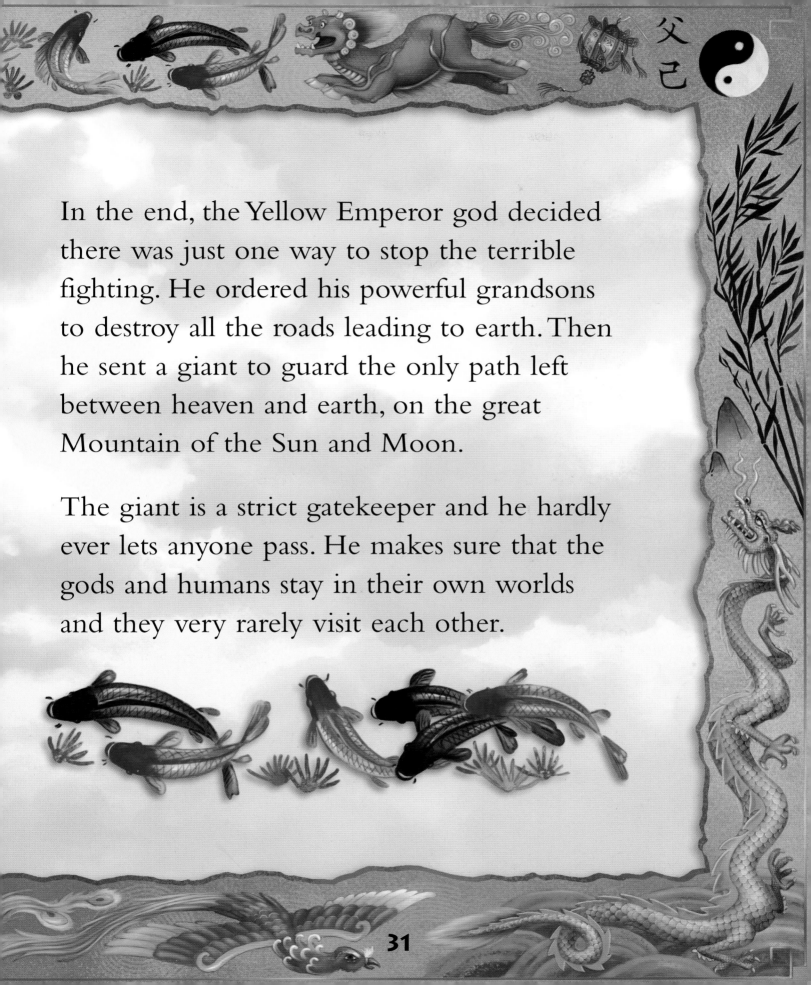

In the end, the Yellow Emperor god decided there was just one way to stop the terrible fighting. He ordered his powerful grandsons to destroy all the roads leading to earth. Then he sent a giant to guard the only path left between heaven and earth, on the great Mountain of the Sun and Moon.

The giant is a strict gatekeeper and he hardly ever lets anyone pass. He makes sure that the gods and humans stay in their own worlds and they very rarely visit each other.

THE MAGIC PEARL

Xiao Sheng and his mother were so poor they could barely grow enough food to eat. Then one year no rain fell on their village. All the crops withered and people began to starve.

Just as Xiao was sure that he would die, he found a pearl, as green and smooth as a pea, hidden in the ground. He took it straight to his mother, who put it safely away in her empty rice jar.

In the morning, Xiao and his mother were amazed to find their jar was full of rice. There was enough for them and all their neighbours. From then on, every morning the jar was full, and they shared their rice with all the villagers.

The news of the magic pearl spread rapidly, and many people were jealous of Xiao. One night, some robbers broke into his house. Xiao knew he had to save the pearl, so he swallowed it quickly. But then he began to feel very strange …

The moment the magic pearl reached his stomach, Xiao felt icy cold. He looked down at his body and screeched in horror. He was turning into a green, scaly dragon!

Xiao ran outside and collapsed on the ground, twisting in agony. Then he fell into a long, deep sleep. When he woke up, he was high up in the air looking down on his tiny mother. Xiao tried to call to her, but huge tongues of flame roared out of his mouth, and she ran away in terror.

Then Xiao heard sweet dragon voices calling him. It was time for the dragons to fly back to their kingdom in the sky. Sadly, Xiao followed his new companions, crying huge tears as he flew. He was very sad to say goodbye to all his human friends, but he managed to leave them one last gift. Where Xiao's tears had fallen, the land became green and lush. The villagers would never starve again.

THE DRAGON AND HIS DOCTOR

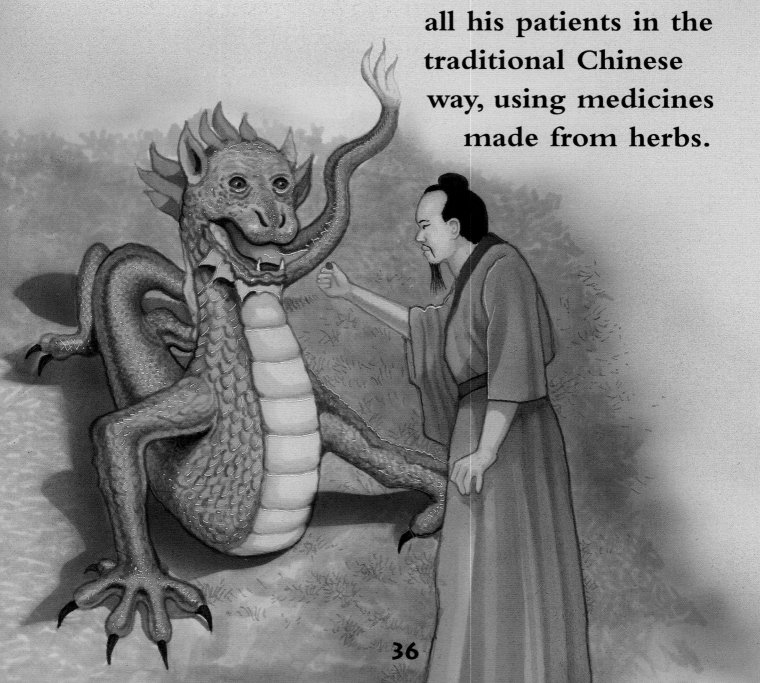

There was once a village doctor who was famous for his skill. He cured all his patients in the traditional Chinese way, using medicines made from herbs.

One day a dragon appeared in the village, roaring fiercely. Everyone else ran away, but the doctor saw straightaway what was wrong. He calmly mixed up his toothache medicine and fed it gently to the dragon. The dragon loved his delicious medicine and made a very rapid recovery. He became great friends with the doctor and visited him every day.

It wasn't long before news of the dragon had spread, and crowds of people came to stare at him. This made the doctor very sad, because he liked to lead a quiet life. The dragon saw that his friend was unhappy, so he asked him to climb onto his back. Then he flew straight up to heaven.

The doctor was very happy in heaven. He lived a peaceful life there with his dragon friend, growing heavenly herbs and giving medicines to the gods.

THREE WILD BEASTS

Zhou Chu was very strong and brave, but he had a terrible temper. Everyone in his village was frightened of him. Then one day, a priest set him a challenge: Zhou had to fight three wild beasts.

Zhou was very proud of his strength so he happily agreed. He set off boldly to fight the first beast, a man-eating tiger. The tiger was extremely wild, but Zhou strangled it with his bare hands.

For his second challenge, Zhou had to overcome a fire-breathing dragon. The dragon had killed many people, but Zhou plunged his axe straight into its head.

Zhou was now ready for his third task, overcoming the fiercest beast of all. He wondered what terrible monster this could be, and he was amazed to learn that the fiercest beast was Zhou himself.

Zhou thought very hard about the priest's challenge, and he realized that he was indeed a monster. Suddenly he felt very ashamed. He decided to take on the hardest task of all, mastering his own temper.

THE LION DANCE

Many years ago, a group of villagers were preparing to celebrate New Year when they heard some terrible news: a fearsome monster was lurking in the hills. Every night it crept into the village and seized a child.

The villagers did not know what to do, so they asked their animal friends for help. First they called on a cunning fox to chase the monster away, but the monster quickly gobbled up the fox. Then they asked a tiger for help, but the tiger ran away and hid in a cave.

Finally the villagers asked a lion if he would fight the monster. The lion was very brave and he did not hesitate. He raced up into the hills roaring loudly and shaking his mane. The monster had never seen such a frightening sight and it ran away as fast as it could.

When they heard that the monster had gone, the villagers were delighted, and the lion became a local hero.

For a whole year, the villagers enjoyed a peaceful life, but then the monster returned, just in time for the New Year's festival. This year the lion was far away, guarding the emperor's palace, so they had to face the monster alone.

At first the villagers were desperate. But then someone had a bright idea. If they dressed up as a lion, perhaps they could frighten the monster away.

Everyone set to work to make the lion costume. They made a long body and a massive head with staring eyes and pointed teeth. Then they practiced a fierce lion dance.

On New Year's Eve, the monster crept into the village, but the villagers were ready for it. Dressed in their scary costume they charged at the monster and frightened it away. Then they had a celebration dance through the streets.

Today, Chinese people still dress up in a lion's costume every New Year's Eve. And they still perform a lion dance to frighten any evil spirits away.

WHO'S WHO IN CHINESE MYTHS

CANJIE

Canjie is a minor god who works for the Yellow Emperor. His job is to keep a record of everything in heaven and earth. Canjie showed humans how to write by drawing symbols that represented objects. In the Chinese language, the word canjie means a written symbol.

CHANG ER

Chang Er is sometimes known as Chang'e or Ch'ang-O. She was the human wife of Yi, the archer. In the Chinese legends, Chang Er flew to the moon and turned into a toad, but later she became the goddess of the moon. At the time of the autumn full moon, people worship Chang Er at open-air altars.

DIJUN

Dijun is also known as Di Jun. He is a god who lives on the outer edge of the Great Eastern Sea, where the sun rises every morning. Dijun married Xi-He, the goddess of the sun, and she gave birth to ten suns.

FIVE EMPEROR GODS

Five powerful emperor gods ruled in heaven. The emperor gods were coloured yellow, blue, red, white and black. The chief god was Xuan Yuan, the Yellow Emperor, who ruled over the earth. Fushi, the Blue Emperor, was the ruler of the woods and was also in charge of spring. The powerful Red Emperor controlled fire and winter, the White Emperor ruled over autumn, and the frightening Black Emperor was in charge of winter.

PANGU

Pangu is sometimes known as P'an ku. He was the first spirit and he created the sky and the earth. Chinese artists usually show Pangu as a hairy giant with horns on his head.

NUWA

Nuwa is often known as Nu Kua. Nuwa is the younger sister of Fushi, the Blue Emperor god. She is the spirit who created humans. She is shown in Chinese art with the head of a woman and the body of a snake or a fish.

YI

Yi is sometimes known as Ho Yi or Archer Yi. He is a minor god who worked for the more important gods, hunting and shooting down evil spirits. For a while Yi lived on earth and had a human wife called Chang Er.

GLOSSARY

bamboo A plant with tall, hollow stems and long green leaves.

buffalo A kind of ox, with large, heavy horns.

chariot A vehicle with two wheels that is usually pulled by horses.

dam A tall wall, built to hold back water.

dragon A fire-breathing monster with a long tail and a scaly body.

emperor The male ruler of a very large country, or group of countries.

lava The boiling hot, liquid rock that pours out of a volcano when it erupts.

magpie A black and white bird with a large beak.

Milky Way The wide band of stars that stretches across the night sky.

mould Model or shape something.

potion A drink that can work magic.

shrine A building that is made specially for a god.

spirit A powerful creature that is not human.

symbol A sign that stands for something else.

torrent A large amount of flowing water.

tradition A way of doing things that has stayed the same for hundreds of years.

transform Change into something else.

vein One of the many tubes that carries blood around the body.

wilderness A large area of very wild land.

Yang In ancient Chinese beliefs, Yang is the light, bright, masculine force that makes up half of the world. (The other half is made up of Yin.)

Yin In ancient Chinese beliefs, Yin is the heavy, dark feminine force that makes up half of the world. (The other half is made up of Yang.)

FURTHER INFORMATION

BOOKS

Ancient China (DK Eyewitness Books) by Arthur Cotterell and Laura Buller (Dorling Kindersley, 2005)

Chinese Fairy Tales by F H Martens (Dover Publications, 1998)

Chinese Myths and Fantasies by Cyril Birch (Oxford University Press, reprinted 1996)

Five Heavenly Emperors: Chinese Myths of Creation by Song Nan Zhang (Tundra Books, 1994)

Traditional Stories from China by Saviour Pirotta (Hodder Wayland, 2006)

WEBSITES

firehorseportfolio.com/tea/
A collection of Chinese legends and folk stories

www.livingmyths.com/Chinese.htm
A retelling of the Chinese creation myth, with some useful background information on Chinese religion and the meaning of the myth

www.educ.uvic.ca/faculty/mroth/438/CHINA/chinese_new_year.html
An illustrated site on the Chinese New Year festival

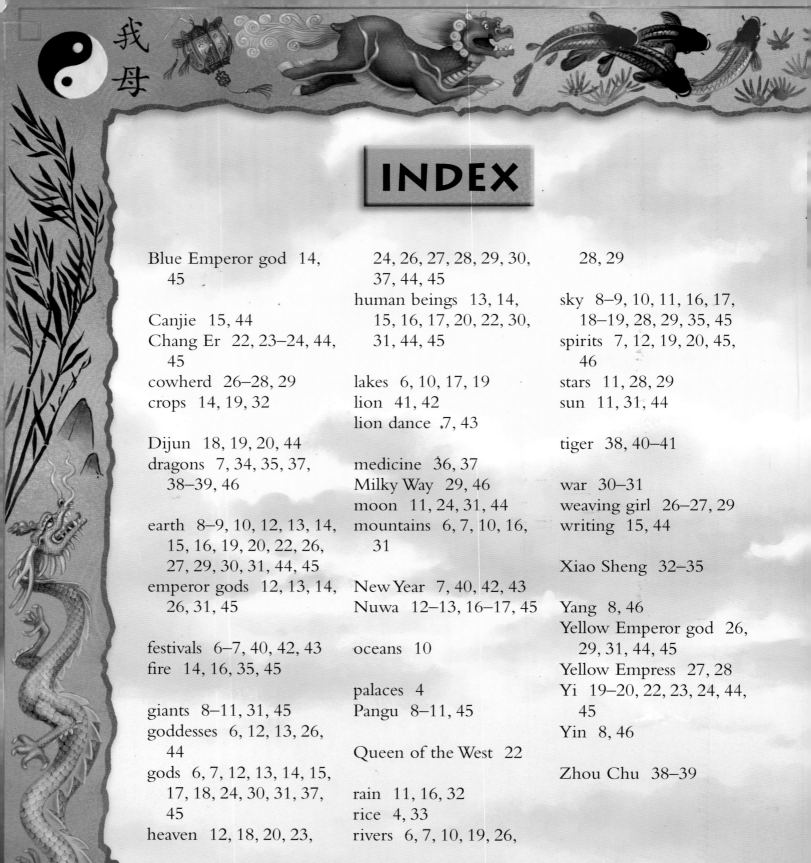

INDEX